## DATE DUE

# Mama Dug a Little Den

## a Little Den

Jennifer Ward illustrated by Steve Jenkins

Beach Lane Books   New York London Toronto Sydney New Delhi

Mama dug a little den
beneath a fallen tree.
An earthy home as soft as moss,
a nursery for three.

A red fox mother digs
a maternity den—a
place specifically to
give birth to her kits.
The father fox will
supply food to the
mother and kits, but
he does not enter the
den.

Mama dug a little den,
then tucked herself away
to pass the chill of wintertime
and days so bare and gray.

*Hibernaculum* is the term for a place that
animals use to "sleep" through the chill
of winter, when weather is extreme and
food is scarce. (In Latin, it means "tent for
winter quarters.") Land toads create a
hibernaculum by burrowing deep in soil. They
remain there through the winter, keeping snug
below the earth's frost line.

Mama dug a little den
within a bubbling stream.
A rugged lodge of sticks and twigs
where we could grow and dream.

Beavers build a den, or lodge,
within a water source by
harvesting tree branches and
logs with their teeth. Entry to
the lodge is underwater and
leads to dry chambers above.
Both parents raise their kits,
who remain with them for two
years. Yearlings help maintain
the lodge and babysit new
offspring.

Mama dug a little den,
a furrow in the ground.
She hid a nut down in its depths
so it would not be found.

Red and gray squirrels "scatter hoard," gathering and burying nuts in small holes they dig in the ground all over the place. They use their great sense of smell to locate their stashes, digging to retrieve their snacks. If a buried nut is left behind, it may grow into a new tree.

Mama dug a little den
in tree roots dark and damp—
a river house with walls of mud
so we could swim and camp.

The platypus, an egg-laying mammal, digs
a den for nesting and resting near water.
Females lay one to three eggs that hatch in
about ten days. Once hatched, the young
nurse for up to four months and then swim off
to live on their own.

Mama dug a little den,
a cave of sparkling snow.
She kept us close and warm and fed
while winds outside would blow.

The female polar bear digs a maternity den, a large hole in a snowbank. Here she will live for several months, giving birth to her cubs and caring for them completely on her own. Cubs venture out of their den for the first time at about four months of age and stay with their mother for almost three years.

Mama dug a little den
to hide out from the sun—
since baking in the desert
isn't fun for anyone!

In the Sonoran Desert,
one of the hottest
deserts in the world,
animals must adapt
to survive the extreme
heat. The desert's Gila
(HEE-la) monster uses
a burrow year-round,
remaining in its depths
when temperatures are
highest and venturing
out when the sun isn't
too intense.

Mama dug a busy den
that spanned across the land.
A crowded place with many pals,
and tunnels, far and grand.

Prairie dog families create a huge network of underground burrows, called towns. Their burrows contain nurseries for babies, places for sleeping, and even areas they use as a toilet. Other animals inhabit these burrows too, including snakes, owls, and black-footed ferrets (which hunt prairie dogs!). The largest known black-tailed prairie dog town covered 25,000 square miles in Texas and was home to approximately 400 million prairie dogs!

Mama dug a little den,
a place to hide and wait
for some great feast to wander by
and meet its final fate.

Most species of tarantula are burrowers. Although many spiders spin webs to catch prey, tarantulas do something different. They wait inside their burrows for a potential meal, such as a cricket or grasshopper, to pass by and then they ambush it.

Mama dug a little den,
and even with its smell,
our home was cozy, snug, and safe;
we babies loved it well.

Skunks sometimes dig a den, but they usually find an abandoned one created by another animal and then line it with leaves and grasses. It will be used year-round for resting, hiding, birthing, and raising two to twelve kits.

Mama made a little den
of hillside, brush, and boulder.
We pounced. We purred. We called it home,
until we grew much older.

A mother bobcat creates a maternity den in
a place such as a hollow log, boulder shelter,
cave, or depression in a hillside that buffers and
protects her from weather and predators. There
she'll give birth to one to six kittens, who remain
with her until they're almost a year old.

Mama dug a little den
along a river's bluff.
We stayed inside our grassy nest
till I grew strong and tough.

Excellent at digging, armadillos create several dens to retreat into when feeling threatened. Females dig a maternity den where they give birth to one to twelve babies, called pups. Pups nurse for two to four months, maturing between nine to twelve months of age.

Mama found a little den,
a hiding place for sleeping.
And each day as the sun would set
we bunnies took to leaping.

Eastern cottontail rabbits, unlike their European cousins, do not dig dens. They may find and use an abandoned burrow, or they may scratch a shallow den, or "form," among weeds and brambles. The den offers shelter for resting and for raising young.

Mama dug a sandy den
beneath the pale moonlight.
She laid her eggs within its depths,
then buried them out of sight.

A female sea turtle leaves her ocean home to come ashore and lay her eggs, usually at night. She digs a sandy cavity to lay them into, then covers them with sand and returns to the sea. Burying the eggs helps to maintain the proper temperature necessary for hatching and protects them from predators.

Perhaps *you'll* come across a den,
dark and deep and wide . . .

and it will make you wonder
who or what might be inside!

## A Note from the Author

When Animal Planet's television program *Backyard Habitat* suggested I create a Certified Wildlife Habitat for the Gila monster in my Arizona backyard, I was hesitant—but only for a split second. After all, how wonderful would it be to have this elusive, fascinating reptile find shelter in our yard?

Over the years, my backyard has been home to a variety of animals that burrow and den, including the Gila monster (of course!), tarantulas, bobcats, snakes, and a myriad of other creatures. Today I share my Illinois yard with foxes, rabbits, skunks, moles, and many other species.

Once one takes the time to look around outside, dens and holes seem to appear everywhere—from tiny anthills in a sidewalk's crack to larger openings in a wild hillside. It's easy to take them for granted and not even give them a second glance. Yet every single den an animal creates or uses serves a specific purpose and is necessary for the animal's survival.

I used the term "mama" loosely throughout this book, as sometimes holes, dens, and burrows are excavated by females, sometimes by males, and sometimes by both.

It may be challenging to determine what animal is responsible for every hole or den one may encounter. So look for these clues:

### Location

Is the den near a water source? Up in a tree? Near a house or civilization? Out in the wild? Knowing habitat basics often provides hints to the type of animal that may have made the den.

### Size

Holes smaller than your thumbnail were most likely created by an insect, crustacean, or arachnid, such as a yellow jacket, small crab, or wolf spider. Insects and spiders excavate some of the smallest dens you will find.

### Other Evidence

Look closely at the area around the den. Are there footprints? Tracks left by an animal's body or tail? You can also look for leftover food scraps and scat. Of course, practice safety and respect when you come across a den. Never enter a large den or place your fingers, hands, or feet inside a smaller den—not only for your own protection but because this is the home of another living animal and the place it relies upon for survival.

Animals and their dens—they're mysterious and fascinating!

Want to dig deeper? For additional resources and creative, STEAM-focused lesson plans, visit my website: JenniferWardBooks.com.

For Andrea Welch
—J. W.

For Robin Page
—S. J.

BEACH LANE BOOKS
An imprint of Simon & Schuster Children's Publishing Division
1230 Avenue of the Americas, New York, New York 10020
Text copyright © 2018 by Jennifer Ward
Illustrations copyright © 2018 by Steve Jenkins
All rights reserved, including the right of reproduction in whole or in part in any form.
BEACH LANE BOOKS is a trademark of Simon & Schuster, Inc.
For information about special discounts for bulk purchases, please contact Simon & Schuster Special Sales at 1-866-506-1949 or business@simonandschuster.com.
The Simon & Schuster Speakers Bureau can bring authors to your live event. For more information or to book an event, contact the Simon & Schuster Speakers Bureau at 1-866-248-3049 or visit our website at www.simonspeakers.com.
The text for this book was set in Garamond.
The illustrations for this book are collage.
Manufactured in China
0618 SCP
First Edition
2 4 6 8 10 9 7 5 3 1
Library of Congress Cataloging-in-Publication Data
Names: Ward, Jennifer, 1963– author. | Jenkins, Steve, 1952– illustrator.
Title: Mama dug a little den / Jennifer Ward ; illustrated by Steve Jenkins.
Description: First edition. | New York : Beach Lane Books, an imprint of Simon & Schuster Children's Publishing Division, [2018] | Audience: Ages 3-8. | Audience: pre to grade 3. | Includes bibliographical references and index.
Identifiers: LCCN 2017042147 | ISBN 9781481480376 (hardcover : alk. paper) | ISBN 9781481480383 (e-book)
Subjects: LCSH: Animals—Habitations—Juvenile literature. | Animal behavior—Juvenile literature.
Classification: LCC QL756 .W37 2018 | DDC 591.56/4—dc23 LC record available at https://lccn.loc.gov/2017042147